ISBN 978-1-7329351-1-2 (Paperback)

Library of Congress Control Number 201-89-12767

Written and Illustrated by Lewis Satini
Editor by Cathy Lynn Bryant

Printed by Lewis Satini Publishing Studio, LLC., in the
United States of America.

Second edition 2018.

Lewis Satini Publishing Studio
115 Dover Furnace Rd
Dover Plains, NY 12522

Planting
A Kingdom
Seed

Written &Illustrated by

Lewis Satini

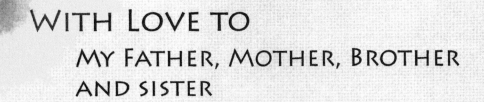

WITH LOVE TO
MY FATHER, MOTHER, BROTHER AND SISTER

THANK YOU FOR ALL YOUR LOVE, SUPPORT, COURAGE, AND FOR THE MANY YEARS WE SPENT TOGETHER. I MISS YOU ALL. REMEMBER, YOU ARE ALWAYS IN MY PRAYERS.

ONCE UPON A TIME,
the father had three children.

ONE DAY,
The father called for them to gather together.

HE SAID,
I will give you these seeds. It is up to
you what you do with them. I will come
back to see the fruit you have grown.

ONE OF THEM,
put the seeds in their offering box.

ONE OF THEM,
put the seeds in their house.

ONE OF THEM,
dug in rich soil and planted the seeds.

ALL OF THEM FAILED,
except for the one who planted in rich soil.

THE FATHER CAME
and rewarded the one that brought forth fruit.

HE INSTRUCTED THE OTHERS
to pray and plant beside God's flowing river, so their plants might be continually refreshed and their leaves would never wither.

EVERYONE STARTED
working hard together planting their seeds,
and the father watered them daily.

SHE SAID,

"This will be my garden,
I'll plant with care.
The sun will shine.
The rain will fall.
The seeds will sprout
and grow up tall."

IN THE HEART OF THE SEED,
buried so deep,
a tiny seed,
lay fast asleep,
"Wake up!" said God,
"And glide to the light,
of raindrops bright,
the little seed heard,
and it rose to see,
the wonderful miracle of God.

AND GOD BROUGHT THE SUN
and the wind, the sun shone
brightly and gave strength to all.

IT RAINED AND RAINED.
For God brought forth the rain
to water the seed, then, the seed
began to sprout.

IF WE REMAIN FAITHFUL,
when summer comes we will
see beautiful creatures, called
butterflies, which will dance
around - rejoicing and praising
God for His glory and His
beautiful creation.

BUT WHEN AUTUMN COMES.
all the plants leaves will
fall to the ground, and rabbits
will come out to find food.

YOU WILL HAVE TO WAIT
through all the winter days to
see the leaves reappear...

WHEN SPRING COMES AGAIN,
the trees will fill out
with leaves of gold
and green.

THE TREES WILL AGAIN SOAK
in the summer sun and rain.

WHEN GOD BRINGS AUTUMN AGAIN,
He will whisper on the wind.
The wind will dance,
and you will hear the sweet lovely
sounds of God's creation.

AND IF YOU WAIT AND PRAY,
season by season, year by year...

THAT TREE WILL GROW SO LARGE.

it will hold you, and...

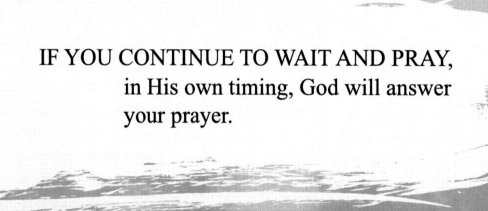

IF YOU CONTINUE TO WAIT AND PRAY, in His own timing, God will answer your prayer.

AFTER THE TREE GROWS,
we wait for the fruit to come.

SOMETIMES WE NEED
to cut down branches
that don't bear fruit.

BY CARING
for the trees in that way,
the fruit will be able
to fully grow.

AND THEN IN
HARVEST TIME,
 we will reap
abundantly.

GOD MAKES ALL THINGS GROW.
He teaches His children to plant
in rich ground so that their
seeds will bear fruit.

SO, AS WE KEEP ON SOWING.

We shall surely reap
a bountiful harvest in
our lives from God's
eternal seeds.

THE FRUIT SHALL BE READY
in its season, freely given out
to those whose lives are
sowing seeds.

Thank You.

God loves you

Born Lewis Satini on January 17,1979, in Medan, Indonesia. Lewis Satini is an illustrator and designer.

Lewis Satini earned a BFA in Computer Animation from Academy of Art University. As an illustrator and designer, he is well-versed in myriad traditional and digital media.

Lewis Satini was inspired by the life of Jesus Christ. As a follower of Jesus Christ, he wish the story to reflect the very basis of the life of Christianity and that the story glorifies His Name and His beautiful creation. He wish that all the children around the nations will know the story of Jesus Christ.

fb.com/lewissatinipublishingstudiio/

lewissatini.art

Made in the USA
Columbia, SC
04 February 2020